priddy bicknell
big ideas for little people

This book was made by Roger Priddy, Joanna Bicknell, Robert Tainsh, Jo Douglass, Louisa Beaumont. Richard Brown and Steve Shott took the pictures.

Copyright © 2001 St. Martin's Press
175 Fifth Avenue, New York, NY 10010

Published by priddy bicknell
A division of Macmillan Publishers Ltd.

All rights reserved, including the right of reproduction in whole or in part in any form.

10 9 8 7 6 5 4 3 2

Manufactured in Malaysia

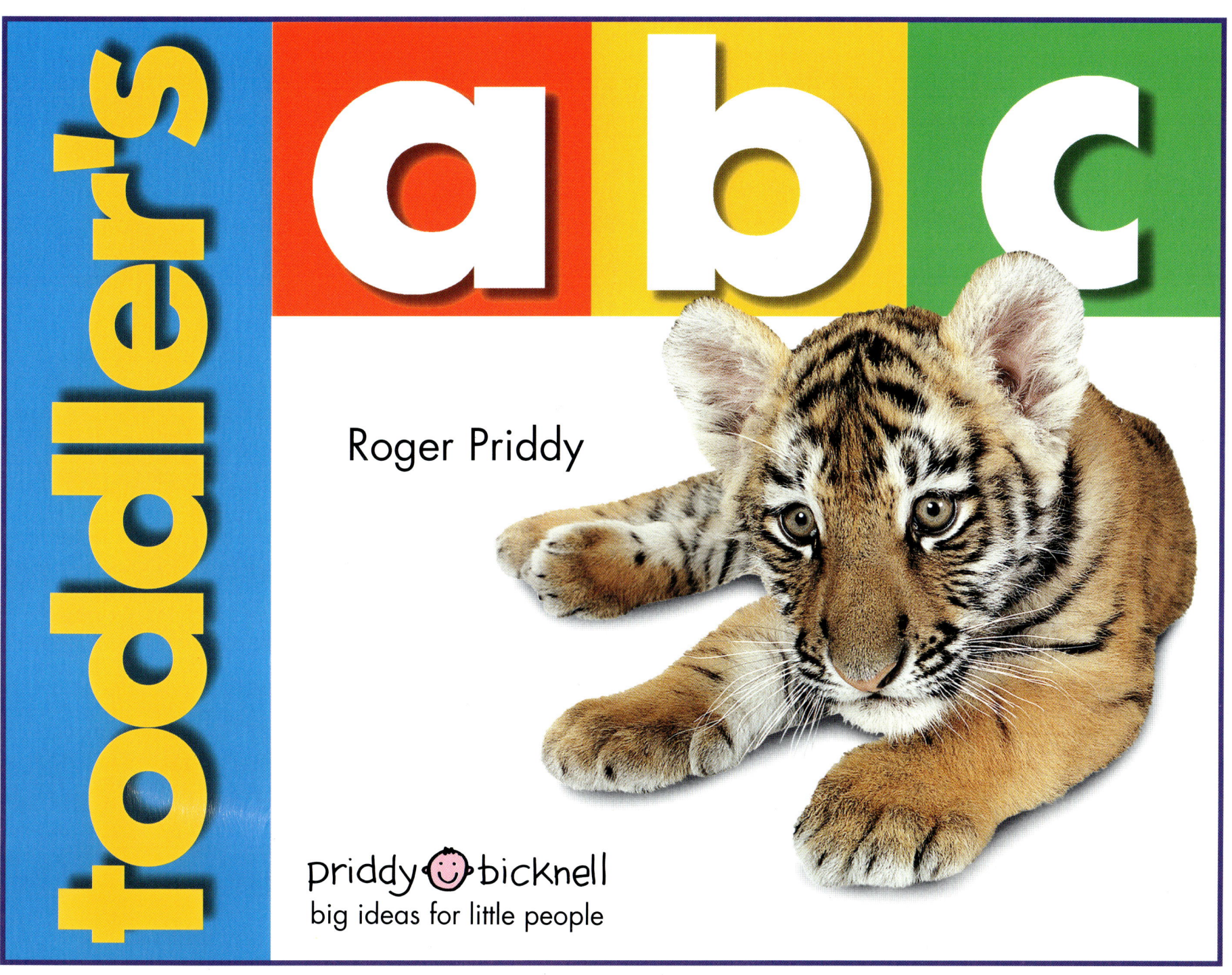

I spy with my little eye, something yellow.

How many animals can you see?

I've got a very long trunk. What am I?

elephant

eagle

Yes, I'm an elephant!

f

feet

fire truck

face

fish

fruit salad

flower

frog

My babies are called chicks and I live on a farm. What am I?

I spy with my little eye, something red.

Can you see anything on this page that can fly?

I

lamb
lamp
ladybird
leaves
lemon
lizard
lion

I'm a colourful bird that squawks! What am I?

What is pink and has a curly tail?

I'm a very tall flower with yellow petals. What am I?

macaw

n

nose

numbers

o

orange

owl

I'm a noisy macaw!

I'm a sunflower!

How many wheels can you count?

table

tiger cub

tractor

telephone

tomato

Which of these objects makes a sound?

How many animals can you see?

w
washing machine
watch
watering can
wolf

x
xylophone
y
yacht
z is for...

zebra

my alphabet

a b
c d e f g h
i j k l m n
o p q r s t
u v w x y z